The Beaver's Lodge
Building with Leftovers

by Adam Reingold

Consultant: John Hadidian, Ph.D.
Director, Urban Wildlife Programs
The Humane Society of the United States

BEARPORT
PUBLISHING

New York, New York

Publisher: Kenn Goin
Editorial Director: Adam Siegel
Creative Director: Spencer Brinker
Design: Dawn Beard Creative
Photo Researcher: James O'Connor

Library of Congress Cataloging-in-Publication Data

Reingold, Adam.
  The beaver's lodge : building with leftovers / by Adam Reingold.
    p. cm. — (Spectacular animal towns)
  Includes bibliographical references and index.
  ISBN-13: 978-1-59716-872-4 (library binding)
  ISBN-10: 1-59716-872-6 (library binding)
  1. Beavers—Juvenile literature. 2. Beavers—Habitations—Juvenile literature. I. Title.

QL737.R632R45 2010
599.37—dc22

                    2009011723

For more information, write to Bearport Publishing Company, Inc., 101 Fifth Avenue, Suite 6R, New York, New York 10003. Printed in the United States of America.

10 9 8 7 6 5 4 3 2 1

Contents

A Very Big Discovery

On October 2, 2007, Canadian scientist Jean Thie (TEE) was studying **satellite photos** of Earth on his computer. He looked very carefully at a photo that showed **wetlands** in Canada's Wood Buffalo National Park. Suddenly, something in the photo caught Jean's attention. He zoomed in to take a closer look.

The world's longest beaver dam (shown in yellow) is about three feet (.9 m) high and four feet (1.2 m) wide. Few people have seen it because it is far from any roads or trails.

Jean saw a large object stretched between two wooded areas. As he studied the photo, he was shocked to discover that he was actually looking at a huge beaver **dam**. "To find a 500-meter (1,640-ft) dam is not that hard," Jean said, "but 850 [meters] (2,789 ft) is quite amazing!" In fact, Jean had discovered the longest beaver dam in the world. It was longer than nine football fields placed end to end!

North American beaver

Beavers are the largest member of the **rodent** family in North America, which also includes squirrels, mice, and rats. The furry builders can grow up to four feet (1.2 m) long.

Nature's Builders

The dam that Jean Thie discovered is located in western Canada. Yet beavers build dams all across North America, as well as in parts of Europe and Asia. Why do the furry **engineers** make them?

A beaver family, or **colony**, usually needs a **pond** where it can build its home. Most of the time, beavers don't go out and look for ponds. Instead, they make them using water from a river or stream. To do that, they first need to build a dam.

Beavers in the Wild

Arctic Ocean

ASIA

NORTH AMERICA

EUROPE

Atlantic Ocean

Pacific Ocean

AFRICA

Pacific Ocean

SOUTH AMERICA

Indian Ocean

N

W   E

S

AUSTRALIA

There are two kinds of beaver—the North American and the Eurasian beaver.

Southern Ocean

ANTARCTICA

☐ Where North American beavers live

☐ Where Eurasian beavers live

Instead of building a home in a pond, some beavers dig a home, called a den, into the side of a river or lake.

Beavers make a dam out of branches, logs, and mud. The dam stops the flow of water from a river or stream. The blocked water behind the dam spreads out over the nearby land and forms a pond. Now the busy animals can start their next project—building the family's home, or **lodge**.

A beaver family can build a dam in about a week.

beaver pond

dam

A pond created by a beaver dam is usually home to one beaver colony.

Home at the Lodge

To stay safe from land **predators**, beavers often build their home in the middle of a pond. They carefully construct their dome-shaped lodge using the same materials they use to build dams—branches, logs, and mud. They pile up the materials until they are higher than the surface of the water. When the busy builders are done, the finished lodge can rise more than 6 feet (1.8 m) above the pond.

dam

pond

food pile

tunnel entrance

Inside the lodge, a beaver colony lives in one large room, or chamber, that sits above the water. Tiny holes in the lodge's roof let fresh air into the chamber. The colony sleeps in this room during the day. The resting beavers huddle together in warm, dry nests made from grass and tree bark. They also raise their young in this room.

lodge

chamber

young
beavers

tunnel
entrance

Beavers build dams and lodges as well as gather food mostly at night. Doing this helps them stay out of sight of predators such as wolves and coyotes.

Meet the Family

Each beaver colony is made up of one male and one female adult and their young, called kits. In the spring, the adult female gives birth to between one and four tiny kits. Over the years, a colony can grow to have as many as ten beavers.

This mother beaver cares for her young kits in the colony's lodge.

At about two years old, each kit will leave its pond to start its own colony with a beaver from another colony. A kit may travel more than 150 miles (241 km) to find another beaver to **mate** with.

Beavers work hard for their family. The adult female cares for kits that are less than a year old. Both adults work with older kits to gather leaves and tree bark for food. Older kits and adults also have another very important responsibility. They repair holes to make sure the dam doesn't leak and the lodge doesn't **flood**.

This adult beaver (right) and kit (left) eat plants in shallow water. Beaver kits often start to swim within a few days after they are born.

Building with Trees and Leftovers

Humans use cement and steel to make and repair buildings. Beavers, however, use supplies that are near their pond, such as logs and branches. They also build with leftovers, such as sticks they have partly chewed for food. They may even use soda cans, tires, and other garbage left by people.

To get their main building supplies, beavers chew down trees and cut them into sections with their sharp teeth. They drag the tree logs and branches, along with the leftovers they find, to the pond.

Beavers cut down trees of all different sizes. Some trees, such as poplar trees, can be more than 5 feet (1.5 m) wide and up to 120 feet (36.6 m) tall.

Once in the water, these strong swimmers push their supplies to the dam or lodge. Then they make a pile with them, one piece at a time. To finish, they spread mud over the materials to hold them tightly together.

It takes about two or three days for two adult beavers to build their home.

This beaver packs mud on its lodge to make it strong.

A beaver can work up to 12 hours a day and cut down more than 200 trees in a year. That's why a person who works a lot is said to be "busy as a beaver."

Food for All Seasons

Building dams and lodges is a tough job. Beavers must eat a lot to get the energy they need to work. During warm months, these plant-eaters munch on plenty of tree leaves and pond plants such as water lilies.

Beavers enjoy eating the bark of aspen, willow, poplar, maple, and other kinds of trees.

Beavers don't eat the whole tree. They usually eat just the inner layer of bark and the tree's leaves.

In the cold winter, beavers rarely leave their ice-covered pond and cozy lodge to find food. Instead, they eat the tree branches that they cut down during summer and fall. The branches are piled in the water and held in place by the mud on the bottom of the pond. This supply of food is called a **cache**. During the winter, beavers can easily swim under the frozen pond to reach their cache for a tasty meal.

lodge

cache

A beaver colony's cache is stored in the pond, close to its lodge, during the winter. The cold pond water keeps the branches fresh

Built for the Job

Beavers are fairly small animals. Luckily, they are built to cut down and move the tall trees they need for building. For example, the front teeth on a beaver are large and sharp. They are strong enough to gnaw through trees, cut branches, and strip bark. In addition, a beaver's front paws can grip objects such as branches that need to be moved.

With its sharp front teeth, a beaver can chop down a tree that is six inches (15 cm) wide in a few minutes.

A beaver's orange-colored front teeth never stop growing. Chewing on tree bark wears down the teeth and keeps them from getting too long.

Other parts of a beaver's body also come in handy. A thick, flat tail supports the animal while it stands on its back feet to cut down trees. The paddle-shaped tail also steers the beaver when it moves branches and logs in the pond. Webbing between the toes on a beaver's back feet helps push the strong swimmer quickly through the water.

Beavers have wide, paddle-shaped tails that help them swim.

A beaver's webbed back foot

A beaver's brown fur is very thick. The fur keeps the animal warm and protects its body from sharp sticks.

Sending a Message

Beavers are usually peaceful animals. However, they are **territorial**. The furry creatures protect their colony from animals, including other beavers, that they don't want near their home.

To **communicate** with outsiders, they build **scent mounds** around their pond. The scent mounds are made of mud and a chemical paste, called **castoreum**, that the beaver makes in its body. The strong smell from the castoreum warns beavers from other colonies to stay away.

scent mounds

Scent mounds act as "no trespassing" signs to beavers that aren't from the area.

Until the 1700s, castoreum was used by Europeans as a medicine to treat headaches and fevers. With its burnt-orange smell, castoreum is still used today to make perfume.

Beavers also communicate using sounds. If a beaver senses danger, it slaps its tail on the pond's surface. This makes a very loud noise. Other beavers in the colony hear this warning and plunge into the pond. After they disappear underwater, they swim to their lodge.

This beaver creates a big splash when it slaps its tail on the water.

Unfriendly Neighbors

When there is danger, beavers are safest in their lodge. The water surrounding their home keeps away predators that cannot swim.

There is one predator, however, that can swim into the beaver's lodge—an otter. A beaver colony can fight off an otter attack, though, if it works as a team. It can also escape through one of the lodge's underwater tunnels.

The beaver is an expert swimmer. It can stay underwater for up to 15 minutes without coming up for air.

In the water, adult beavers are rarely attacked. Why? They are fast swimmers! Beavers can swim up to six miles per hour (9.7 kph). On land, however, they are no match for predators like cougars and bears. Beavers may swim quickly, but they **waddle** slowly on land.

This grizzly bear has killed a beaver.

A cougar hunting a beaver

In the wild, beavers live for about 10 years. In the safety of zoos and animal parks, they can live for more than 20 years.

Changing the Land

Beavers aren't large in size, yet they have a big effect on their **environment**. When beavers make a pond, water plants such as duckweed and cattails begin to grow in and around the water. Lots of insects such as mayflies and dragonflies move to the pond. They lay their eggs on these water plants and in the still pond water.

After beavers make a pond, many kinds of plants begin to grow there.

No other animal can change its environment more than the beaver except for humans.

Frogs, turtles, and ducks then come to feed on the new plants and insects. Raccoons arrive to eat the eggs in the nests of ducks and turtles. Larger animals like moose also come to eat water plants. In this way, beavers create new wetland **habitats** for many plants and animals.

Leopard frog

Wood duck

Beaver habitats are home to many animals, including leopard frogs, wood ducks, and moose.

Moose

Beavers in Danger

Many people admire beavers for their hard-working ways. Yet people have also hunted them for different reasons. Today, beavers sometimes build dams in **culverts**, which are human-made tunnels that allow roads to be built over small creeks. When beavers clog a culvert with a dam, the creek waters rise and can flood the road. To prevent this from happening, some people try to kill the beavers in the area.

A road was built on top of this culvert so that people could cross over the water below.

In the past, people hunted beavers for their fur. Beginning in the mid-1500s, hats and coats made from beaver fur became popular in Europe. Hunters killed millions of beavers in Europe and North America. By the early 1900s, the animal was almost **extinct**.

Warm hats and coats made from beaver fur were very popular in Europe from the mid-1500s to the mid-1800s.

Beaver skins must be stretched out and dried before being made into hats and clothing.

In the early 1700s, beaver skins were used as money to trade for goods. One adult beaver skin was worth two pounds (1 kg) of sugar or two shirts. A gun was worth 132 beaver skins.

Beavers Are Back!

By the 1900s, beaver fur had become less popular to use for hats and coats. As a result, fewer beavers were hunted. Laws were also passed that made it illegal to hunt them. Luckily, the animal was saved from extinction. However, after many years of being hunted, some areas where beavers had once lived now had no beavers at all.

Today, scientists are **reintroducing** beavers to habitats where they once built their homes. They hope this will create wetlands and help the beaver **population** grow in those areas.

In 2007, a beaver was discovered living in a lodge in a river in New York City. It is the first wild beaver to be found living in the city in more than 200 years!

These beavers are being reintroduced in Scotland. Because of overhunting, it has been about 400 years since wild beavers lived there.

Because of these efforts, the beaver population is now getting bigger. About 20 million beavers live in North America. More than 600,000 live in Europe and Asia. With a little help, these eager builders can continue to create habitats for many years to come.

Beaver Facts

North American beavers are a type of rodent. They are very social animals that live together in family groups called colonies. Here are some more facts about North American beavers and their amazing colonies.

Length	Head and body: 30–36 inches (76–91 cm) Tail: 9–13 inches (23–33 cm)
Weight	usually 30–60 pounds (14–27 kg)
Fur Color	reddish-brown or brown
Food	plants such as water lilies and clover, and trees such as aspen, poplar, and willow
Habitat	North America, except parts of southwestern United States, southern Florida, and arctic regions
Kinds of Buildings	dam; free-standing lodge in a pond; less commonly, a lodge attached to the side of a pond; and tunnels and dens built in the sides of rivers and streams
Colony Population	up to 10 family members
Life Span	about 10–12 years

More Animal Towns

Beavers are not the only rodents that work together to build spectacular homes. Here are two others.

Nutria

- Nutria are large rodents that live mostly in South America, and also in parts of Canada and the southern United States. They grow to be about 36 inches (91 cm) long, including their tails. They weigh between 10 and 20 pounds (4.5 and 9 kg).
- Nutria live in wetlands. They eat mostly plants and roots.
- Colonies include a male, several females, and their young. Colonies can have up to 13 members.
- Nutria dig their homes, or burrows, underground in the sides of rivers, marshes, lakes, and ponds.
- The burrows contain rooms up to 3 feet (.9 m) across. They are used for feeding, sleeping, staying safe, and taking care of young.

Nutria dig their underground homes near rivers and lakes.

Naked Mole Rat

- Naked mole rats are small rodents with very little hair and strong jaw muscles. They measure about 3 inches (7.6 cm) long, including their tails, and weigh between 1 and 2.4 ounces (28 to 68 g).
- Mole rats use their powerful jaws to burrow through the dry soil of eastern Africa, searching for food and building tunnels. They spend most of their lives in the dark rooms and tunnels that they dig.
- Naked mole rats live in colonies that consist of 20 to 300 individuals. Each colony has one queen and one to three breeding males.

Naked mole rats live underground in eastern Africa.

- Other colony members serve as soldiers and workers. Soldiers protect the colony from predators. Workers maintain the colony, gather food, and care for the queen and her young.

Glossary

cache (KASH) a hidden supply of food that is stored for later use

castoreum (kast-OR-ee-uhm) a chemical paste produced by beavers that is used to mark their territory

colony (KOL-uh-nee) a family of beavers; it includes an adult pair that mates, and their young

communicate (kuh-MYOO-nuh-kayt) to share information

culverts (KUL-vurts) tunnels that allow roads to be built over small bodies of water

dam (DAM) a strong barrier built across a stream or river to hold back water

engineers (en-juh-NIHRZ) people who design and construct buildings

environment (en-VYE-ruhn-muhnt) the area where an animal or plant lives, and all the things, such as weather, that affect that place

extinct (ek-STINGKT) when a kind of plant or animal has died out; no more of its kind is living anywhere in the world

flood (FLUHD) to overflow with water

habitats (HAB-uh-*tats*) places in nature where plants or animals normally live

lodge (LOJ) a beaver home, usually built in a pond that was formed by beavers

mate (MAYT) to come together to have young

pond (POND) an enclosed body of water that is smaller than a lake

population (*pop*-yuh-LAY-shuhn) the total number of a kind of animal living in a place

predators (PRED-uh-turz) animals that hunt other animals for food

reintroducing (*ree*-in-truh-DOOSS-ing) bringing animals back into an area where they once lived

rodent (ROH-duhnt) a small mammal with long front teeth, such as a mouse, rat, or beaver

satellite photos (SAT-uh-*lite* FOH-tohz) pictures taken by a spacecraft that orbits Earth, the moon, or another heavenly body

scent mounds (SENT MOUNDZ) piles of mud and chemical paste that beavers build to communicate with other animals

territorial (*ter*-uh-TOR-ee-uhl) having a strong desire to defend an area against intruders

waddle (WAHD-uhl) to walk slowly and awkwardly, usually by taking small steps and swaying from side to side

wetlands (WET-landz) marshy lands

Bibliography

Burde, John H., and George A. Feldhamer. *Mammals of the National Parks.* Baltimore, MD: The Johns Hopkins University Press (2005).

Müller-Schwarze, Dietland, and Lixing Sun. *The Beaver: Natural History of a Wetlands Engineer.* Ithaca, NY: Comstock Publishing Associates (2003).

"Beaver Natural History Narrative." National Park Service. **http://64.241.25.182/glac/forteachers/beaver-natural-history-narrative.htm**

"Beaver." Alaska Department of Fish and Game. **www.adfg.state.ak.us/pubs/notebook/furbear/beaver.php**

Read More

Kalman, Bobbie. *The Life Cycle of a Beaver.* New York: Crabtree Publishing Company (2007).

Mara, Wil. *Beavers.* New York: Marshall Cavendish Benchmark (2008).

Marie, Christian. *Little Beavers (Born to Be Wild).* Milwaukee, WI: Gareth Stevens Publishing (2006).

O'Sullivan, Elizabeth. *Beavers.* Minneapolis, MN: Lerner Publications (2007).

Learn More Online

To learn more about beavers and their lodges, visit **www.bearportpublishing.com/SpectacularAnimalTowns**

Index

About the Author

Adam Reingold has written books about communities, history, and science. He lives near the East River in New York City with his wife, Jennifer, and their Portuguese Water Dog, Monkey.